More than Before

A First-Generation College Student Guide

Katelyn Cano

MORE THAN BEFORE

A First-Generation College Student Guide

By: Katelyn Cano

Cover Design by Megan Rohrer

ISBN: ISBN: 978-1-387-22837-9

In Memory of Noelle

PROLOGUE

One day in fourth grade, my teacher was predicting what college the students in my class would attend. When he got to me, he said I would go to Davis. Davis never happened, but being told I could go to college, for the first time in my life, changed everything. I was unable to forget being told about the positive results that could happen after someone obtains a college degree. I heard a degree could get one a job they liked. A job that made them never have to wonder where their next meal would come from. A job that could give someone the ability to remove the word broke from their vocabulary. A job that would make it so their kids would never have to feel the burden of being alive, which was something I felt often since I knew how much I cost. For a long time, I concluded my family would be better off financially if they did not have to pay for things I needed to survive. For me, fourth grade was when the college dream exploded in my heart, mind and spirit.

The dream grew the way it did because of several things I observed from a young age. For the majority of elementary school, I did not see Kathy, my mother, as much as everyone else seemed to see their mother and the lack of time with her upset me more than anything. I saw Kathy for a couple hours in the morning before she drove my brother and I to school and headed to one of her jobs. After school, my brother and I would hang out, skateboard and argue until Ivan, our father, picked us up and we went to his house until he drove us back to Kathy's house the next morning. As my brother and I called Kathy in the evening to say goodnight, she was finishing up her last hour at that job and getting ready to head to her graveyard shift of waiting tables. Both of her jobs barely made ends meet and I felt this every single week, or when I opened the fridge and there was almost no food before payday. This was a battle I knew I did not want when I was "old." I also wanted to do something I loved as a job. I knew Ivan and Kathy were not fired up about what they did for a living; so, discovering I could become whatever I wanted after studying was exhilarating. To put it more simply, I just wanted out of what I was born into, so from nine and beyond, I took that grain of knowledge about college, what it could produce, held onto it and never let go.

Sometime during September 2006, when I was 17 years old, I began to make my college dream become a reality, and I applied to colleges. It was an undercover mission since I did not tell my family what I was doing. I did not tell them for two reasons. First, we still had financial battles. I knew that me leaving to get an education would mean the money I was contributing would have to go to my education instead of the family. Kathy hoped I would be promoted from a courtesy clerk to a cashier at the grocery store where I worked, so I hid my college plans. Second, I knew my family would be unable to help me with my college applications. Both issues were a challenge, but having no help from Kathy, Ivan, or my brother was the greater problem of the two. It made my college application process overwhelming and I remember dreading a lot of it since I had no idea where to begin at all. I was about to become the first one in my immediate family to finish high school, and that made attending college seem extremely far away and near impossible.

As a first-generation college student, I did not have the luxury some classmates had of being able to go to a parent for advice, wisdom, or even a $55 college application fee. I had no idea where to find scholarships. I did not understand grants and loans. I did not even know that there were over twenty California State University campuses. In addition, the lack of emotional family support was astounding. All of this made my journey to college incredibly chaotic and bewildering.

As a decade passed, I was in graduate school and discovered I was not the only first-generation college student to be crushed, and confused. In fact, the California State University system reported in 2016, that one-third of their students were first-generation college students (CSU 2016). Discovering there are thousands of high school seniors who share this experience I once had led me to search the web and see if there was a handbook for first-generation college students. I found a lot of books about how colleges can try to help first-generation college students who commonly fail and several other depressing titles. I was only able to find a handful of books that were specifically for first-generation college students and some were just books to help them once they began college, or small snippets of experiences from other first-generation students who had already succeeded.

After this disappointing and discouraging search, I decided there needed to be a book addressing more than the college application essay, or financial aid because going to college is way more than writing a paper and finding grants. The journey to and through college is a process, which needs a foundation of support most first-generation college students do not have and cannot obtain without extensive pursuance. Diana, who is my high school friend's mother, was one of the instrumental people who helped me decide on where to attend college. She once told me that an eighteen-year-old person needs their parents' help more than a five-year-old person because they are stepping into many unknowns that can be complicated and daunting. I remember looking at her and telling her I was fine, yet I was truly not fine at all. I was lost like many other students who have been lost and need support from trustworthy adults who can help in ways their parents may be unable to help. I wrote this book because I want first-generation college students to have a book I wish someone could have given me. I hope this book is practical, and helpful, while also being inspirational and meaningful.

INTRODUCTION

On January 18, 2012, I traveled to London by myself because I had always wanted to be inside of the British Museum and I also wanted to see a Chelsea Football Club match live. My trip was made easy from months of searching on the Internet and the ease of booking a hostel, flights and a trip to Stonehenge. The entire trip was planned from start to finish and I had a perfect road map. In fact, I never steered away from the path I had planned for myself. I could do everything I wanted to do. The trip was easy except for the time I got lost on the way to St. Paul's Cathedral. I made a wrong turn and as I kept walking, I had a gut feeling I should not have been where I was. This was quickly confirmed when I encountered a scary woman who yelled, "Move along, Chelsea!" I was wearing my new Chelsea Football Club jacket, which is why she called me that.

Looking back, I see that applying to college was terrifying like the moment I was walking down the wrong street in London. It was not easy. I had no roadmap. I did not know where I should go. I do not want you, or any other first-generation college student to be as lost as I was. I hope this book can be a roadmap for you. I want it to be the book I wish I had when I was you. When I had no idea how to apply to college. When I did not know the difference between a grant and a loan. When I had no idea how I could ever go to college.

In this book, I will draw from my personal first-generation college student experience to address everything I once needed help with, while also sharing some of my own stories. I am going to be honest and not hold back with any of these examples because I want this book to be authentic and effective. I want you to know you are not alone and I hope you can learn from my journey. This book is split into three different sections. Part 1 is for high school seniors, Part 2 is for college students and Part 3 is for college graduates. This book will have more than just the basics of a college application though. I will share things with you I longed to know and you may not think are relevant, but I assure you they are.

Part 1 includes chapters on building a support system, deciding which type of college to attend, financial aid, college applications and choosing which college to attend. Part 2 will discuss choosing your major, school-work-life balance, guilt many people like you and I have felt and how to graduate. Part 3 are my thoughts on graduate school and your future career. My goal is that you can pick up this book and get all the information you need in one place, or only take what you need, when you need it. Today is the time that first-generation college students, like you, who may have grown up with almost nothing, can discover that you are worth more, and can attain things that were once out of reach, especially a college education.

Lastly, I realize the college journey and reasons for wanting to pursue a degree after high school are unique to each person. The fact you have made it this far into the book shows you have something driving you forward. The biggest thing for me, that I had to remember every time I thought about quitting, was that I was still alive and I knew there was something out there for me. Right after my first birthday, I spent 32 days at Stanford Hospital. On the 16th day, doctors told Kathy and Ivan to prepare for my death. I am, obviously, not dead. I do not remember anything about my life-saving surgery, almost dying, being discharged and re-learning how to walk. What I do remember, is looking at a huge scar on my abdomen as a child and strongly believing it meant there had to be something out there for me besides living in the painful environment I described in the Prologue. I firmly knew not dying meant there was something on the other side. Whatever reason you have for picking up this book and pursuing your education is something I recommend you think about every time you want to drop a class, take a semester off, or downright give up. That fuel driving you in the college process will always help you. Ponder it often.

PART 1

YOUR SENIOR YEAR
OF HIGH SCHOOL

CHAPTER 1

BUILDING A SUPPORT SYSTEM

I rode my bike up to my porch one Spring day after school and saw a large envelope sticking out of my mailbox. I knew from experience a small envelope was a college rejection letter, while a large one was an acceptance package full of information and a congratulatory letter. I wanted to cry and was ecstatic as I opened that envelope from Johnson and Wales University in Denver, Colorado. Shortly after I received my acceptance letter that joy was gone because Kathy told me the university only accepted me because they wanted my money. As a private university, that school was incredibly expensive. For a while, I believed those poisonous words. I was just hurt. The biggest thing I learned was just because someone is a biological relative or friend did not mean I could trust them to guide and support me regarding my higher education plans. I was moving into uncharted territory, and my friends and family from my past could not be my guides. They did not know the way. They especially did not want me to make the journey. It is a painful feeling to hear words like that from someone you love, but I have come to find words like this can exist in the lives of people like you and me. Lack of family support is not a rarity for many first-generation college students. Luckily, the emotional and even financial support every college student needs can be found outside of the family. I am starting the book with this chapter because I believe that having a support system is without a doubt the most important part of anything you will ever experience in life, particularly the high school and college journey. Trust me on this.

Like some first-generation college students, you probably love your independence. You might be grateful textbooks had examples so that you could teach yourself everything like I did for years. Therefore, a support system may not be something you thought you would need to create, or even want. I totally understand because I was that person for too long, but I was lucky enough to eventually realize I needed a lot of help. In fact, self-sufficiency is inefficient when it comes to college applications and attendance.

Diana was the first person I had for support regarding my college goals. There are not enough good things I could say about her and her family. Her parents and her siblings also helped me. When I was a junior in high school, her parents drove me home from a party and asked me all sorts of questions about college. I told them all about my dream of studying forensic anthropology at California State University, Chico. Talking about a college program in depth with them was a beautiful moment for me because it was a conversation I had wanted to have for a long time, but I had no one in my family to have it with. It also got me more excited about going to college and it no longer seemed like a distant concept. These conversations continued with Erin and Kevin, who are the next two people I unintentionally added to my support system. I had more conversations about college with Erin and Kevin than I ever had with Kathy and Ivan and they are still involved in my life today. The other people who regularly supported me during my last two years of high school and my first two years of college were several coworkers from Raley's Supermarket, specifically Rachel, who is still one of my closest friends. Like the others, they are still huge cheerleaders of mine. Whenever I go back to Raley's and visit any of them, I end up in the store for over an hour updating all of them about my life. While I was bagging groceries, most of them always said to me, "Do not be like me and work here your entire life" and they are excited I took their advice. Let me be clear, there is nothing wrong with working in the grocery industry as a career, but I knew and they knew staying at Raley's forever was not my destiny. If you are reading this book and working a minimum wage job, staying there forever is most likely not your life path either.

Since I left my home in Pleasanton, California for college, I no longer had these people to encourage me daily. If you are like me and decide to move away to attend a college, you should be sure to find supportive people wherever you move. I discovered this the hard way because there were still a lot of questions I had during my last two years of college, and I could no longer easily visit Diana. Having people who are even just interested in what you are studying, writing papers about and asking how many semesters you have left is also huge. Al and Laura are the two main people who fall into this category for me and like the others they are still around, which is fantastic. Al and Laura continued what Erin and Kevin started. I love all four of them dearly and see them as the parents I always dreamed of having when I sat in my room as a kid wondering how my life would be if I had a different family. Having Al and Laura during my junior and senior year of college was probably the greatest thing that came out of my move to San Francisco, California. We had many meals talking about my classes, which was a new thing for me. I never had family who cared about the topics of my papers I was writing. Especially when they were about early human time periods most people find dull. They talked to me about the low number of jobs for archaeologists, and why I should get an MBA. These conversations were not discouraging in the way the words of Kathy and Ivan said were. They were conversations out of the love and care they had for me since they did not want me to struggle like I had in the past. They even discussed my plans after graduation and so much more. Now our conversations consist of my plans for my career and my current job I would not have if I had not taken their advice.

The wisdom these kinds of people can offer you is huge, so you should find these people and never lose contact with them. You will find having a consistent group of people for support will be your greatest source for inspiration, help, guidance, and love. All of which are invaluable for your success in college. I can guarantee you will not survive college without a support system, or you will just barely survive.

Lastly, and sadly, you may find your family may be upset if you end up spending more time with these newfound people than them. I have taken an immense amount of criticism due to the time I spend with Al, Laura, Erin and Kevin. It has made family members angry and yours might become angry too. All I can tell you with certainty is that the time spent with the people in your support system is worth it. It is better for you to be filled up by your support system than sucked dry from your family during a time when you are busy and most likely already exhausted from your studies. Do not be concerned with how your family perceives you right now. Remember that your college education will benefit the future generations of your family more than it will hurt the ones who are around today.

Also, my favorite reason for the support system, is that it can shatter your paradigms. I remember being a child and truly believing that life would never get better. If I could go back and visit seven-year-old Katelyn, I would tell her life will get better and make sure she believes it. I thought most humans were terrible and unkind. All those nice characters in movies and books were just characters to me. I never believed there were people on earth who could love in such a way that people like Al, Laura, Erin and Kevin love. I was jaded when I moved into my dorm in San Francisco. I am now thankful the people in my support system have changed my views on humanity and given me a hope I never thought I would have.

CHAPTER 2

COMMUNITY COLLEGE VS. FOUR YEAR UNIVERSITY

I often found myself looking at every piece of paper that came in the acceptance packet I received from Johnson and Wales University. I spent my last couple months of high school and the summer that followed thinking about how great it was going to be to live somewhere where it snowed, was incredibly far away and new to me. A place where I was not abused and demoralized sounded lovely, which is partly why I chose a college far away. All those reasons were why I chose Johnson and Wales University over the other universities that had accepted me. I was excited and ready to have the full university experience, but also terribly confused about how I would ever afford a private university. During this time, I was also living with Diana. Occasionally, Diana would put the local community college's catalog and promotional flyers in my stack of mail. I diligently ignored all of Diana's advice and catalogs she put in my mail pile. I did this because my dreams of living in a dorm and my pride were way too big. I was on a humongous soapbox proclaiming I was better than a community college because of my grades in high school and it is a miracle I ever got off said soapbox. When I saw a community college catalog, all I could think about were the people who slid by in high school, or barely made it. I often recalled a conversation I had with my best friend, Noelle. When we were freshmen, we talked about how the only thing one needed to go to a community college was a high school diploma and discussed our big college plans. I felt like I did more than just earn a high school diploma. I thought I deserved and earned a place somewhere better than any community college. I thought those who did the bare minimum were the only people who went to community colleges and I was NOT one of those people, so I envisioned myself some place fancier.

I waited until the middle of August 2007, to look through all the documents Johnson and Wales University had given me to find their phone number. I felt like I was on hold forever when I was being connected to the admissions department. After finally being connected, I told the admissions employee I was not going to attend because the cost was too high even with the scholarship they offered me. She was upset about the news and wished me the best of luck. In those days that followed, I was crushed and felt like a failure. I reevaluated my options and decided to pursue my passion for cooking by attending The Art Institute in San Diego. This was mostly because I was still on my soapbox and only wanted to go because I was still against the idea of community college. Shortly after I made that decision, Diana stood in the doorway of the guest room I lived in and told me about how some universities in California offer culinary degrees and how expensive it would be to live in San Diego. Erin also hinted at going to community college every time I babysat her boys. It looked like community college had finally become my only option and a couple months later, I found myself searching for late-start classes at the local community college.

I lost out on living in a ridiculously overpriced dorm my freshman and sophomore year of college and commuted to Las Positas College instead. However, it was one of the best decisions Diana and Erin ever encouraged me to make and I do not regret it at all. The annual estimated fees of attending one of the California State Universities are $5,500, while a community college is around $1,200 and these numbers do not reflect living expenses, or textbooks. Since you are a first-generation college student, the financial burden of college is probably great. Thus, I highly recommend the community college option. You may save yourself over $8,000 during your first two years of college if you start at a community college. Financial aid is also readily available for community college students, not just students who start at four-year universities, so you may save yourself even more money by starting at a community college. In addition, some community colleges are becoming tuition-free. City College of San Francisco became tuition-free in January 2017 and other community colleges may offer this in the future as well.

When I started attending Las Positas College, all I could think about was everything I lost out on. Things like living in a dorm, moving to another state, not having to deal with transferring and some other things I honestly cannot even remember now. Looking back though, I see a lot more things I gained. The biggest is, of course, the amount of money I saved, which lead me to see community college as a place for students looking to save money and not just the students looking for an easy alternative. I was also able to keep my job at Raley's instead of having to move and find a new job somewhere in Colorado.

If you are still deciding on whether to attend a four-year university, or a community college after you finish high school, I highly encourage you to go the community college route because of the cost difference. Second, transferring is not complicated, or scary. In fact, keeping track of the classes you need to transfer is very easy. Most community colleges have a checklist you can print from the school's counseling department web page that will show you the number of classes you need to take. In addition, counselors love helping students with advising on classes. It is their job, so be sure to take advantage of what the community college has to offer. I never sought advising, instead I grabbed everything from the school's website. My pride and independence issues were huge at that time. I would have saved myself a lot of time if I had met with a counselor. Having a counselor is also a great person to add to your support system especially since your parents may be unable to tell you what you need to do to transfer.

I strongly urge you to check out your local community college's website during your senior year of high school. If you have any friends attending one, ask if you can sit in on one of their classes to see how it is. If you have an idea of what your major will be, see if they offer an associate degree in that field. You do not have to get an associate degree to transfer, but having a few of the classes you will need for your bachelor's degree is very helpful. Lastly, please do not ever be embarrassed, or ashamed about attending a community college. I was for a very long time, which was a waste of my time and energy. You are not a loser for attending community college. You are someone who is making a financially wise decision while also taking the first huge step for your future.

CHAPTER 3

THE COLLEGE
APPLICATION PROCESS

Deciding Where to Apply

You probably have a lot of reasons why you want to go to a certain college. Some people choose Harvard because it is where their parents want them to attend. Some people, like myself, choose somewhere far away because they want a new experience and want to leave where they came from. Others do not want to leave their family and choose the college in the city they already live. Whatever your reasons are, remember it is the place you will be for two, or four years depending on where you begin, so choose wisely.

The first thing you must decide is whether you want to start at a four-year university, or a community college. Hopefully Chapter 2 helped you make that decision, but if you are still uncertain, then you can apply to both types of schools. This just takes a bit longer, but is a fine choice if you are undecided.

The next important factor to think about is the majors the college offers. The majors offered are less relevant if you are starting at a community college, unless want to get an associate degree from that school. If you want to transfer to a four-year university with an associate degree, then you will need to research the majors the community college offers. The reason the major is irrelevant if you are not getting an associate degree is because you will take the core classes for your major during your last two years of college. Therefore, your first two years at a community college can be used to get the required general education and transfer, which is what I did. Information about majors can easily be found on the website of the college you would like to attend. I encourage you to read about different majors while you are on a school's website and read about the faculty in the academic departments. Also see if the university reports the kinds of jobs that alumni have taken since graduating. If you have not chosen a major, make sure you choose a college that has majors you could see yourself studying. You do not want to end up at a university that does not have anything you would like to study.

I will discuss ways to pay for college in more detail in Chapter 5, but cost is another huge factor in deciding where you should apply. If you are going to need a loan, which I imagine you will as a first-generation student, then it may be best not to choose the most expensive school you would like to attend. It is valuable to know the cost differences between the types of universities in your state. If you are applying to a college outside of your state, then be sure to check the cost difference for out-of-state students. It is usually an astronomical increase in cost and is something you must be aware of. Tuition costs are easily accessible on the website of each college you are thinking about attending, so look at them and compare them with the other schools on your list.

The last important thing to remember is to know who you are as an applicant. It would have been a waste of time and money for me to apply to Yale. An Ivy League school was way out of my reach, and that is okay. Not everyone is an Ivy League bound person and you have nothing to feel bad about if you are not either. Be sure to understand the minimum requirements of each school that you send an application. If you are way below the minimum admission requirements, then do not spend time applying. Putting in time to make a great college application for a school you qualify for is way more valuable than hoping you get into a school like Stanford. Keep in mind as well that there are minimum standards universities list for applicants to have, but most applicants will be above those requirements. You will have to think realistically about how much you have beaten those requirements when you think about your acceptance. Also remember to have a back-up school. This is the school in which you greatly exceed the minimum qualifications and are confident you will get into. Back up schools are necessary in case the schools you would love to attend reject you. Getting denied from your top school may not happen to you, but it is normal and you should be prepared for rejection.

The Components of a College Application

Application Organization

Once you decide where to apply you can start on your applications. At first you may be overwhelmed to find that one school needs a letter of recommendation, but not the others. You will probably also have some schools that want an essay and others that do not. It is completely impossible to keep track of all this information in your head. Trust me, you will end up having your letter of recommendation sent to the wrong place if you do not have it written down somewhere. You should put together a checklist of the materials each school requires. As you complete each piece of the application, you can check it off the list so that you know what you have left to do. The most important part of these checklists is having deadline dates next to each item on the list. Dates are the most important thing to remember for your college applications since nothing can be late. I have heard of many first-generation students and their parents missing deadlines because they are not used to the strict deadlines of college. In high school, you may have been able to turn in something late. This will never be the case for a college though, so keep a detailed checklist for what each college needs and dates of when these items are due.

Letters of Recommendation

I sat in my high school counselor's office one day during March of my senior year to ask her for a letter of recommendation. It was only my second time ever meeting her. She did not know anything about me and I was not happy to be there. You may be a lot like me and are independent and hate asking people for help. Most first-generation college students are like this since their parents may have worked a lot, or their parents could never help them with certain things. If you are accustomed to doing everything by yourself and totally dislike asking anyone for anything, you *will* need to get over that immediately and not be afraid to ask for a letter of recommendation. It is part of the job for teachers and counselors to write letters and you are not bothering them by asking them for one.

Another big issue with having that school counselor write my letter of recommendation was that she did not know my abilities since I had never gotten to know her before. When you are asking a teacher or counselor, make sure you ask one who knows you well and can honestly write about your academic abilities. Make sure they like you also, otherwise, they may not write a great letter for you. Do you remember that support system I wrote about in Chapter 1? Hopefully you have a couple teachers or counselors in your support system you have a good relationship with since they are necessary for letters of recommendation.

The last part about your letter of recommendation is timing. Go back to that checklist and see when it is due. Make sure you ask the person who needs to write it at least two months in advance. No teacher will enjoy being asked to write a letter of recommendation a week before it needs to be mailed. Most teachers also write these letters for dozens of students and will need the extra time. A letter of recommendation is validation that you are the student you claim to be, so take it seriously, give your writers enough time and get the best letters you can to benefit your application.

Essays

Another written part of your application may be short essays. I will be honest and tell you I did not write any of these when I applied to college. I did, however, write them when I was applying to graduate school, so I now have the experience. The first thing I will tell you is you need to give yourself time to write it. An essay for a college application is not something you should write at 5 a.m. with several cups of coffee the day it is due. Be sure to think about the question, or questions you must write about thoroughly and give yourself enough time to develop an outline, write your essay and revise it. I cannot give you a number of how many days or weeks you will need because everyone writes differently. Know how much time you need and make that time for yourself.

Second, you must be honest and open. Do not hold back. This may be hard for you, but it is crucial. Do not be ashamed to write about how you will be the first in your family to attend a university. In fact, pieces of your personal history may help you stand out and should be included. Remember that you are a unique and exciting applicant and that no one has the same story as you. Brenda Ueland, who is one of my favorite authors wrote, "Everybody is original, if he tells the truth, if he speaks from himself. But it must be from his true self and not from the self he thinks he *should* be" (Ueland 4). No piece of writing can be good if authenticity and details are held back, so do not do it. After all, most essays require you to write about yourself in some way and need to truly be about you and not whom you think the college wants to see. Remember, stories about your life you think are boring or not "impressive" can be interesting to a college admissions officer who is in a different time and place in life.

Most importantly, proofread and revise your essay multiple times. Again, you may have to throw out your super independent lifestyle here because you need to make sure you have someone read your essay. Have this person hold you accountable. Find a reader or two who will tell you to be more honest, or if you held back too much. Again, make sure to correct any spelling and grammar errors.

Standardized Tests

I took the SAT at a university in Hayward and I was not prepared for many reasons. The main ones were that I never spent the money on an SAT help course, or had any relevant books to study from since the cost for those were too high. I also was afraid and embarrassed to ask for help. Remember that support system you read about? That also applies here when it comes to asking for help studying. I also knew I had never been the best test taker and was a better writer. I am the kind of person who would prefer writing an essay over taking an exam anytime. You might be like me and also be a bad test taker. I want you to know it is okay and to remember test scores are not the only way that you are evaluated, but an SAT prep course and asking someone who can help is valuable. See Appendix 3 for standardized test preparation books and websites. In my opinion, the best part about your college application is there are multiple components which allow you to show yourself holistically. If you are a good test taker, then the standardized test you must take is probably not scary for you.

All four-year universities require you to take a standardized test and submit the scores as part of your application. You have two options for the required standardized test, the SAT and the ACT. Be sure to see which one is the better option to take for the schools you are applying to. In 2016, average scores were around 1000 for the new SAT (Zhang 2016) and 20 for the ACT (Zhang 2014), but it is always best to shoot much higher than the average score. The more competitive universities expect scores much higher than the averages. I highly recommend taking a study course, or at least books to study from so you are more prepared than I was. The test is not easy and you need to make time to study for it.

It is also imperative to know the costs that come with standardized tests. In 2016, the cost for the SAT was $43 and $54.50 with the essay portion and the ACT without the writing portion is $39.50 and $56.50 with the writing portion. Again, figure out which one you should take. The cost may be a burden for you, so try and get the fees waived and set money aside for study materials and test fees. You can send your test scores to a small number of colleges for free, but will be charged for any additional universities your scores are sent. You will find applying to college is an expensive task and if you have the same financial difficulties most first-generation college students do, you need to plan how you will pay for tests and fees.

Transcripts

Now that we have discussed the written and test parts of the application, we can dive into the other main way you are evaluated, which is your grades. Grades can be alarming and you may not like your statistics grade (I did not like some of my math grades). The colleges you apply to may not like it either, but hopefully you have great grades throughout the rest of your transcript to balance out your GPA. You will submit your grades in two ways: first you will fill them in on your application and then you will have to send transcripts to prove the grades you reported are true. Make sure you know the number of transcripts you must send to each college. Some colleges want transcripts when you apply and others may only want final transcripts. Remember that checklist I just told you about, this is the kind of detail you need on it. Make sure you send them by the deadline. I also recommend calling the colleges you send transcripts to confirm they have been received. As with the other parts of your application, these may cost money, so make sure you figure out the cost of sending transcripts if your high school has any.

The Online Application

The last part of your college application is easy since it is just filling out your basic information. You will need to provide the essentials like your name, address, and birthdate. If you live in California and are applying to a California State University, you only need to do this one time on CSUMentor.edu. CSU Mentor will save all your basic information and even your grades, so you can send multiple applications effortlessly. See Appendix 1 for which websites you can use to apply to colleges in your state. There are also two great organizations—Coalition for Access, Affordability and Success and The Common Application—that are lead innovators in online college applications. Students can utilize these websites to build their college application and send it to institutions the organizations currently collaborate with. However, not every school you apply to will be done via the same website, so be sure to give yourself enough time to fill out your applications in all the places. Filling in these details can take a while since you need to input all your grades and the classes they are from. Most importantly, like with all the other pieces of your application, know the dates of when the application is first available and the last day you can submit it.

Overall, keep your checklists updated and handy as you apply to different colleges. Make sure you carve out enough time to complete each piece of your application. Begin to set aside money, or figure out how you will pay fees for applications, standardized tests and sending transcripts. If you need help, ask for it sooner than later and do not be afraid to ask for it. You are probably a better applicant than you think and do not be afraid to apply as who you are instead of who you think the college wants to you to be.

CHAPTER 4

CHOOSING YOUR COLLEGE

In Spring 2012, I was working for a performance marketing company during my year off before graduate school. I was eagerly awaiting answers from the three graduate schools I had sent applications. One morning, I received two emails from two of the schools. The emails were full of vague text telling me to go online and check my application status. I immediately knew they were telling me to go online and find out my applications were denied since I received a depersonalized email instead of that coveted large envelope in the mail. Sure enough, I signed on to both university websites to find I had been rejected. I got up from my desk, went to the restroom and cried. I was devastated and again felt like I had not measured up. All those same emotions I had when I called Johnson and Wales University flooded me. On the way to my desk, I told the finance manager the bad news. She gave me the cliché "everything happens for a reason" speech I did not want to hear. Luckily, the third and final school did accept me. This experience made choosing where to get my master's degree easy, but choosing a college may not be like this for you.

First, I need to mention it is okay if your dream school when you applied is no longer your dream school you want to attend. People and circumstances change, so do not feel bad for saying no to a school that said yes to you. As with deciding where to apply, you will need to use some of the same techniques in deciding where to attend. Compare the costs of the schools that accepted you. See which schools, if any, gave you a scholarship. This is the time where you must finally decide if you do want to move out of state, or if you want to stay local. Remember that out-of-state tuition I mentioned in the Chapter 3? Be sure to compare that to the tuitions of the other schools that accepted you.

You may want to go to the same college as your best friend, so I am going to be very blunt and tell you your best friend now may not always be your best friend. In fact, there are very few people I went to high school with I am still in touch with on a regular basis and that is okay for you to do. You will meet hundreds of new people whether you go somewhere with your best friend, or not. Take advantage of the new opportunities and do not feel guilty for attending a different school than them.

As with your friends, remember choosing your college is your choice! Do not let your parents, or other relatives make the decision for you because it is a college they want you to attend. Your college career is *your* college career, not your mother's. I have often found many parents of first-generation college students get to live vicariously through their children and thus have incredibly strong opinions about college majors and institution choices. You may encounter people who want you to go to a certain school, so remember to make the choice yourself no matter what they say. Your support system can also be used for advice when you are deciding which school to attend. It is always good to seek wise counsel for important decisions.

If you have decided to attend a community college, know that you have options. You do not have to be like me and attend the one closest to you. Many of my friends from high school left our city and began at community colleges in other cities like Los Angeles, or San Luis Obispo. Doing this can be great, especially if you still want to have the experience of moving away from home right after high school.

The last factor of choosing where to go to college is related to where you want to live. In college, you have two options: living on-campus, or living off-campus. Many people want to live in dormitories, so they can have the full college experience, and I totally understand since I had those dreams once too. The good news is some community colleges offer on-campus housing, so you still get the experience even if you do not start at a four-year school. The main thing to know about living on-campus is that it is particularly expensive. In fact, it cost me more money to live on-campus while I was attending San Francisco State University than it did for tuition. I know, that sounds ridiculous, but it is unfortunately true. Living on-campus was a fun experience though and I do not regret it. It is not uncommon for a bad roommate situation to arise, but I believe such conflicts can be worked through and this should not discourage you from living on-campus. Another thing about living on-campus is the size of the place where you will be living. Most universities now have apartments on campus that are much larger than the one room dorm you have probably heard of most. I highly recommend the apartment style living so that you can cook your own food as meal plans are expensive and the food is not always great. If you are moving to a new city, living on-campus the first year may be best so that you can adjust to the city and then move off-campus the following year. You will most likely have to share a room since single rooms are sparse. If that is something you do not want to do, I recommend living off-campus and finding your own room.

There are several other benefits to living off-campus. The money you will save is, of course, important. Second, you may not have to move out every year as you do with on-campus housing. Moving at the end of every year is a hassle, so if you can find a space off-campus you can stay in the whole time you are in college, you should do it. Being able to choose your roommates is also a great thing. The year I lived off-campus, I knew what I was getting into since I had met with the people before moving in. You can also stay at home if you want to save the most money. I did this while I was attending Las Positas College so that I could save money and because it was also convenient. Do not stay home out of guilt though. As a first-generation student, you are probably working and may be using some of your money to help your family. If this is the case for you, as it was for me, you may receive a lot of negativity around moving out and wonder if the family will be okay if you are gone. They will survive without you and you can see Chapter 6 to understand how to deal with guilt.

To conclude, the most important thing to do is choose the college that is for you and that *you* want to attend. Do not let others make this decision for you and do not ever feel bad for leaving. Be sure to compare costs of tuition. Decide which type of school you want to attend as soon as you can. Finally, weigh out the pros and cons as they relate to you for living on-campus, or off-campus. Everyone reading this book will have varying situations, so choose the college which works best for your goals, finances and wants.

CHAPTER 5

PAYING FOR YOUR EDUCATION AND EVERYTHING IN BETWEEN

After deciding which college I wanted to attend, I went to a meeting about the university with Ivan. It was two hours of learning about the campus, majors, dormitory life and the incredibly high cost of the tuition. Naturally, I was excited and could not wait to hop on a plane to Denver and start college, but Ivan did not feel the same. He was only staring at the piece of paper that listed the tuition and said it would never ever work. In the end, he was right because I did not go to that college, but his actions and words were discouraging. Like most first-generation college students, there was no money set aside for my education, housing, food, or other expenses that come with higher education. I had to figure out how to pay for it myself. Luckily, there are grants and scholarships, but do not count on them to cover all your educational costs. Much of paying for your education will probably come from loans. Additionally, you must keep in mind that you will need to pay for housing, food and maybe even other surprising things that come along. In this chapter, I will go over financial aid, managing work and school and random expenses.

Grants, Loans and Scholarships

Financial aid is broken into three categories—grants, loans and scholarships. Grants are my favorite, so I will begin with those. The way to get grants is by filling out the Free Application for Federal Student Aid (FAFSA) and this is done through their website, which can be found in Appendix 2. The application is lengthy and you will need one of your parent's tax return information for the application. Your parent's income combined with your income (if you have any) is used to determine how much aid you are eligible to receive. The only way to not use your one of your parent's tax return information is if you are an independent student. I was lucky enough to have an amazing college counselor from Las Posits College write a letter on my behalf before I transferred to San Francisco State University, which classified me as an independent student. There are a few ways to be classified as an independent student and I urge you to consider them, but the most likely reason is that you are over the age of 23. Being an independent student often means you will receive more aid, but it is hard to qualify for if you are under the age of 23. Therefore, be sure that your parents complete their taxes on time because it is best to submit the FAFSA before March 30 of the year you plan to attend college. The longer you wait, the less money there is available. It is best to complete the application in January, if possible. The rest of the application is other personal information, but the most important part is adding the colleges you want your information sent. This is where you search for every college you have applied to and add them to the list so that their financial aid office receives all your information. Even though you will only be attending one of the schools, you need to add all of them since you may not know which one you will be attending while you are filling out the FAFSA.

In addition to providing your grant options, the FAFSA determines the amount of money you are eligible for regarding student loans. There are two types of student loans and they are subsidized and unsubsidized. Subsidized loans are based on your financial needs, you are not responsible for the interest that accrues on them while you are in college and you do not have to begin paying them back until six months after you graduate.

Unsubsidized loans are not based on financial need, you are responsible for the interest that accrues while you are in college, and they also have a six-month grace period that begins after you graduate. If possible, stick with subsidized loans since you will have less interest to pay, but you may need to use an unsubsidized loan depending on the cost of the college you attend. Both loan options available to you are based on the cost of the school's tuition. I have a mix of both types of loans, but thankfully they are not high since I was an independent student. Again, consider this option as it can be helpful.

Once you are enrolled in the college you choose, you can view your financial aid using the online access your college gives you. The college will tell you to accept or decline your financial aid awards. In other words, you decide how much of the money available from grants and loans you want. Grants you do not have to pay back, so be sure to accept all the grants offered. The financial aid page should 'tell you how much your tuition and housing (if you are living on-campus) will cost, so you will know how much money you need. After accepting the grants, you can figure out if you need to take out any student loans and as mentioned before, try to stick with the subsidized loan. This process of applying for financial aid and accepting your awards needs to be done every year you are in college, and is the same process for graduate school.

To add to the money you have for college, you can apply for scholarships. Many scholarships available are specific and require more time than applying for grants and loans. The best places online to search for scholarships are listed in Appendix 2. Scholarship websites typically have a lengthy profile set-up you should complete thoroughly so that you are matched with the most scholarships you can qualify for. There are many scholarships only available to students who belong to certain organizations, ethnicities, religions, etc., so be sure to fill out as much as you can on scholarship websites. The second most important thing to know about scholarships is the amount of time they take. Most scholarships can require transcripts, letters of recommendation and essays. I decided to work on one that required reading Ayn Rand's *Atlas Shrugged*. I am disappointed to say the book was too long and I never finished in time to write the essay for the scholarship. Be sure to set aside enough time to write your essay and get the other documents that are required for any scholarships you apply to. Be realistic with what is required for the scholarship and what you have time to do. I clearly recommend avoiding huge books if you are working full-time and going to school full-time. Also, be sure to have good relationships with teachers, or school counselors who can write letters of recommendation for you. These types of relationships will also come in handy if you decide to apply to graduate school. Another important thing students often overlook is the appearance of their application. If you can, mail your applications in a large envelope so it is not folded up. This is more presentable and easier to open by your scholarship reviewers. Everything you can do to make it simpler for them helps and makes you look organized and professional.

Working Before and During College

The money you receive from financial aid should cover all your tuition and textbook costs, but you will also have to keep in mind how you are going to pay for food, rent and transportation. Living on-campus is costly (see Chapter 4), so if you choose to live on-campus, you will most likely have to use a student loan to pay for it since it needs to be paid in full at the beginning of each semester. It is best to have a job during your senior year of high school so you can begin saving for college with the money you make. If you are like most first-generation college students who help their families financially, be sure you put away money for your education when you can. I had this watermelon shaped money bank—the kind that only open when you break them—I used to put money away in and did not open it until right before high school graduation. Get one of these. Since breaking it to get the cash is the only option, you may be like me and more likely not to break it until you need it.

The biggest effect a job can have on your academics is the time your job takes away from your studies. Be prepared to have to work right when you are done with school and staying up late after work to complete assignments. You will most likely have to work during the weekends also. All of this may sound daunting and it will put a damper on your social life, but the extra money you take into college will be worth it. Due to the time a job takes, you may not be able to get that 4.0 you want. Remember, anything above a 3.0 in high school is good and if you want to go to graduate school then you should keep a 3.3, or above during college. However, some colleges like to know if you had been working during high school and this helps them understand you and your grades better. Thus, having a job while in high school can improve your application for some colleges.

The second most important thing about working in college is finding a job that both pays well enough for you to survive and works with your school schedule. Your class schedule will change every semester/quarter, so it is best to have the flexibility with your job so you can attend your classes. Make sure you are working somewhere that can work with your class schedule and never skip a class to cover someone's shift. Your education comes first, and do not forget that. While I was working at Raley's, I ended up having to work at 3 a.m. so that I could go to classes in the afternoon. I absolutely do not recommend working an early morning shift and then going to class. Whenever possible, go to class before you have to go to work. Otherwise, all your valuable energy will have been used up at work and you will be drained during class. The best option is having class in the mornings and afternoons followed by work in the evenings. I worked this type of schedule during my last two years of college and it was no surprise that my grades were better than my first two years of college. Another key thing to remember is to get your class schedule to your boss as soon as you can. No boss likes a student who tells him his schedule the day before a semester begins.

Most importantly, it is imperative to know you will most likely have to work while you are in high school and in college. Do everything you can to make sure you can have a flexible schedule that works around your classes. Be responsible about going to class and getting there on time. Finally, be persistent at enrolling in morning classes and working in the late afternoon or evenings. I worked full-time during college as well as graduate school. Yes, it was depleting, but I do not regret it since it allowed me to eat and pay for the other necessities of life. This may be your situation. Hang in there because it can prove to be worth it. I promise.

Other and Unexpected Costs

As you have read, Erin and Kevin have done many things to impact my education and life. When I look back, I am reminded of something I never expected to ask them for—money. It was about two months before I moved to San Francisco and I had a housing deposit due since I was planning to live on-campus my first year. This was an unexpected cost that caught me completely off guard. I applied for a small loan at my bank and was denied. This left me sitting across from them one evening at their kitchen table asking for $600. Never in my life had I seen such generosity than that evening when Kevin went to the other room to grab their checkbook with no questions asked. I went on and on about how I would babysit for them for the rest of my life to pay them back. I can tell you they were not concerned about being paid back, and if you have anyone like them in your life, you will find your education and future matter more than money you owe them. This was the first of many unexpected costs I encountered during my college years and I feel it is important to include a quick section about expenses you may encounter.

The first thing you will have to pay for related to your education are textbooks. The days of a teacher handing a book to you the first day of class are over when you enter college. It truly depends on you major and the classes you take, but expect to spend around $400 per semester/quarter on textbooks. I highly recommend not buying textbooks from the bookstore at your college. The prices are typically a lot better when you buy from Amazon, or eBay. You also have the option of buying books new or used. Used books can often have highlights and writing from the previous owner(s), but if you buy used, you can end up saving a lot of money. You can also rent books from some college bookstores and websites, such as Chegg. If you do end up renting, you will be unable to take notes inside the book, so if you are someone who needs to do that to learn, renting may not be for you. You can also sell your books online, or back to the school bookstore when your semester/quarter is over, which can help you pay for the next round of books you will buy. One thing I do recommend is to keep books you think could be useful again. Since I studied anthropology, I kept most of my main anthropology textbooks and used them as resources for future papers I had to write. I especially recommend keeping books that are resources for academic writing, which English classes most often require since you will have to write papers all throughout college and they could be useful again. Lastly, a good dictionary and thesaurus combo will be beneficial for academic writing you complete.

The second expense to keep in mind are living expenses, such as rent and food. As I wrote before, living on-campus is costly, so renting a room is the option I recommend to college students I meet who are not planning on living at home. During one of my college semesters, I rented a living room in an apartment shared with five other people, so I understand living with other people can be hard and frustrating, but it is often the most affordable option. Craigslist is the best website to use to find rooms for rent. Regarding food, find the most affordable grocery store you can wherever you move to. If you work somewhere that provides food, always take advantage of it. During my last two years of college, I was a nanny and ate with the kids and their mom as much as possible. I even strategically paid back Erin and Kevin the money from the housing deposit on Thursdays because that was when Erin made these awesome meals before the boys and Kevin played rugby. I know that story might sound silly, but I must say that every dollar you do not have to spend on something is super valuable and I cannot recommend eating for free whenever and wherever you can. When it comes to transportation, do everything you can to keep costs down. If you are taking public transportation, see if there is a way to get discounted tickets. This is sometimes possible if tickets are bought through a store, or as weekly or monthly passes instead of paying each time. If your school provides a free shuttle, take it.

The best way to plan all your expenses is with a detailed budget. I did not budget properly until I got my job after graduate school. Thankfully for me, Laura is an accountant and helped me out. It is great to put how much money you take in at the top of an Excel file and then all your expenses below. You can use formulas in Excel to calculate how much money you will have after paying your bills. You may encounter unexpected fees like I did, so try to be prepared for those. Please do not wait as long as I did to begin budgeting. If you do, you may find yourself having to drink your coffee black while waiting to get paid to buy coffee creamer. That is a true story of how I became to like drinking black coffee, not a joke. Overall, plan for spending money on rent, utility bills, food, textbooks, transportation, and your cell phone.

PART 2

YOUR COLLEGE YEARS

CHAPTER 6

YOUR COLLEGE EXPERIENCE AND GUILT

I have always loved Easter more than any holiday including Christmas. I love it even more today because of something that happened during Holy Week—the week before Easter—in 2010. During that week, I was full of guilt. I have come to learn it was false guilt, not from anything I had done wrong. False guilt is crushing and mine came from Kathy giving me guilt for something I did not have to feel bad for. In my case, she laid into me before I moved away to San Francisco since I stopped paying rent. After I moved, there were many times I talked to her on the phone where she described her financial struggles. I looked at my nice apartment, my amazing roommates, and this life I was creating with guilt. It is easy to believe you do not deserve anything great if many people treated you as such most of your life. I hope much of this did not and does not happen to you, but if it did or does, this Holy Week story is for you.

Throughout that week, I was feeling down about my amazing life while people were back in Pleasanton still living in the circumstances I was lucky enough to leave. Al knew something was not right and he asked me about it as we were preparing an unreal amount of lamb for Maundy Thursday dinner happening the following day. I let him know my concerns about living in San Francisco and feelings about abandoning my responsibilities in Pleasanton. They were big feelings, and in addition to them, I was surrounded by all these people who loved me and I had no idea how to deal with it. It was like there were Erins, Kevins and

Dianas everywhere. It was new and scary. Someone once asked me how I let Al and Laura into my heart after years of only letting in a few. Two answers: they picked up where Erin and Kevin left off and never stopped loving me. They proved to me repeatedly they were not going to bail. They still have not, which shocks me considering how difficult I was. Along with Al and Laura, these new friends in San Francisco never stopped loving me. There is a saying that a parent's voice becomes a child's inner voice. It happened with me and my inner voice told me I did not deserve all the exploding, unrelenting love. I did deserve it and you deserve love to. All the false guilt finally unleashed on Good Friday when I cried through an entire evening church service. It was crushing me and I knew I had to get to Pleasanton to do something about it even though I had no idea what I would do when I got there.

I got to Pleasanton late that evening after a train ride where I ran into a minister who kept preaching to me about self-condemnation. That is what I call fate since the door to the train I wanted to get on was broken, which lead me to meeting her. Since it was late when I arrived, I headed to my friend's house and decided to see Kathy in the morning. She was going away that weekend, so I knew I had limited time and when I arrived to the house the next day, she was already gone. My mission for redemption was crumbling, so I decided to clean her entire house. After this I only left feeling more guilty. How could I ever be worthy of everything waiting for me in San Francisco if I could not even make up for leaving? That was all I thought. Before leaving her house void of fulfillment and validation, I grabbed my journals from high school. I read them on the train ride back to San Francisco and all they did was confirm San Francisco was exactly where I needed to be. I knew I could not go back to Pleasanton, but I was also terrified to stay in San Francisco. I am thankful every single day I got to the house too late and found my journals instead of a conversation with Kathy. Reading those were corroboration I needed to get back to the exciting life across The San Francisco Bay. Easter is my favorite because it was when I decided to fully say yes to the new life waiting for me and goodbye to the one others tried to force on me and was never meant for me.

If you feel this way after moving away to college, or even just committing more to your education and dealing with such guilt, I will tell you what several people told me. If this is your situation, you need to hear it. You are the child and not the parent; therefore, it is not your responsibility to make sure your parents' bills are paid, they have food to eat, or that your siblings are cared for. Your parents survived before you had a job and they can survive without your help again. Do not delay your life because of false guilt, as this will not be good for you, or your family. You will find living on your own is freeing and you will also probably enjoy being able to finally only take care of yourself. It will be tough and you may be on the receiving end of harsh words and judgement. However, as many described it to me, the living paycheck to paycheck lifestyle is surviving, not living. When you have the opportunity to live, go live.

CHAPTER 7

BALANCING SCHOOL, WORK AND LIFE

The summer of 2010, I worked four jobs. My reason was to avoid pain from my past. In fact, one coworker at one of my jobs asked me what I was running away from. I remember wondering how she knew since she only saw me one day a week and I had just met her. People talk about work-life balance. Mine was just school-work balance. A lot of my life before moving to San Francisco was filled with grief, so why would I want to have more life like that? School and work protected me from all the anguish. But, as you recall from Chapters 1 and 6, life is not all bad, especially if you have the right people in it. Living this way better than surviving. I must say work-life balance is not exact and in fact, not entirely possible. There will be some days where you are in a science lab for eight hours. Other days where you work so hard at your job you have no energy for anything left. School, work and life all have busy times and slow times, so do not be discouraged if you feel like one day you are sitting in a study group for ten hours. It happens and it will not always be that way. What I want you to know is that life can be added in between all the crazy work and school days.

One thing Al and Laura made me do during college was write down everything I did on a calendar. At the time, I believed if it was something recurring, such as work or a class, it should not be in my calendar. But, being who they are, they made me write it all out. I am a bit appalled thinking back to that calendar. It was way too full. There was no life in it. Please do not do this. A big regret I have from my college days is I did not live enough. I did every assignment, studied for every test, worked every extra hour I could and I pushed people away. I look back and I am shocked Al and Laura never gave up on me. They are proof of good and proof of love. Erin and Kevin are also proof of these. I hope you have people like that and be sure not to shove them away. Keep that support system strong and live in it. Spend time with people in addition to the studying and working. You will have time for it if you prioritize it.

During that busy summer, someone told me about a "Joy Bank." The idea is that there should be something you do every day that adds joy to your life. I was caught up in working and my GPA and was bereft of joy for a long time. It was not until I acknowledged the need for a Joy Bank that I put fun things in my calendar. I cannot emphasize the importance of this enough and it is still something I practice today. I hope you choose to add things to your Joy Bank, or do something like it.

More than anything, my biggest life related regret from college that I truly hope does not happen to you, is that I did not celebrate enough. I held this belief that everything I achieved in college was unworthy of celebrating because I did not have a degree in my hand yet. Every finished semester, "A" paper, completed midterm was not qualified for celebration. Nothing on the way to graduation day felt good enough (more of that inner voice I wrote about earlier). My hope for you is you celebrate everything big and small. It is all part of the educational journey and worth the ice cream even if you are eating out of a pint container while watching trashy reality TV. Celebrate it all.

As I wrote before, working full-time and school full-time is tough. Truly the hardest work I ever did and the hardest work you may ever have to do too. I look back and wonder how I was even able to ride my bike to work at 2:30 a.m. and not fall asleep during class at 3:00 p.m. All of it was worth it, but I know now it could have been alleviated a bit had I spent more time enjoying the moment rather than focusing on graduation day. Please soak up everything instead of throwing it out on the road to graduation day and do not let feelings of imbalance between school, work and life unnerve you.

CHAPTER 8

CHOOSING YOUR MAJOR

My first anthropology professor told me she chose her major because it was the first one listed in the academic catalog. I am not sure if this is a true story, but either way, this is not a method I suggest for you. When I was in high school, I thought I wanted to be an archaeologist, and then I wanted to be a cop and then a chef. The truth is that most people do not totally know what they want to be, or they have a lot of ideas and cannot decide. Whichever one of those you are, do not worry because you have some time. During your first two years of college, you will take many classes in distinctive departments to fulfill your general education requirements. While you are doing your general education, you might find you really love political science (if that is even possible) and decide you want that to be your major.

I ended up choosing anthropology because I loved the subfield of archaeology and it was something I was (and still am) incredibly passionate about. I love everything about the Bronze Age, the Philistines, and the Ancient Middle East. I now know that archaeology is not a practical career and I am no longer an archaeologist. Instead, I am now in the field of applied anthropology and finished my master's degree in anthropology with a focus on business anthropology. Although it is important to study something you enjoy, you should also choose a field you know has a job market. This is something I wish I would have known before the first time I discussed it with Al and Laura. I suggest searching job boards to see what jobs you could get based on what you study. Pay attention to salaries and understand how much money you will need to make for the area that you would like to live in after you graduate. If you do not like the salary options, or the jobs you can get with your degree, then you should change your major.

Another important thing Al and Laura taught me was that I could still be involved in archaeology even if I am not an archaeologist. Al once told me that I could make enough money to fund an archaeology dig, or travel to archaeology sites if I got an MBA instead. The day he told me that, I came home angry, thought he was completely wrong, threw my bag on the ground and said, "He is an idiot." I truly believed I could never be satisfied if I was not physically in a trench digging. However, in summer 2015, I took a vacation to Easter Island where some of the most mysterious archaeology exists. I can assure you I was satisfied. During that trip, I remembered what Al had told me as I was hiking a volcano. I laughed at how silly I was thinking I had to dig to be happy and was forever grateful to Al in that moment. You should think about ways you can still be involved in something you love even if you do not get a degree in it.

You should also know you do not have to become what you study. I know it sounds crazy, but there are a lot of companies looking for people who have a bachelor's degree and it does not matter what it is in. My first job after college was for a performance marketing company and it had nothing to do with archaeology, obviously. It was having a degree and the skills that come with it and not my marketing knowledge that got me the job. If you are interested in boosting your resume and willing to work in different fields from the one you studied, that is totally fine. I do think it is important to study something you generally like and find interesting. Do not force yourself through a business program if you despise business. It will not work and you will dread going to class every day. Whenever possible, take classes you see yourself enjoying, or classes related to what you do love.

If you decide to pursue a major you love, you should figure out how many years you will need to be in college. It is near impossible to find an anthropology job with just a bachelor's degree, and the same can be said with psychology. Keep that in mind when you are deciding what to study. If you know right now you want to be a doctor, then you need to understand immediately how many years of college you will need. If you want to be done in four years, do not study anthropology. See Chapter 10 to learn about graduate school.

The first two years of college, no matter how many years you plan to study, will be dominated by the general education classes I mentioned earlier. These classes are the foundation of your college experience. You will find you have categories of classes you need to complete and each category has many classes from which to choose. If you know your major, choose classes from that subject that can help fulfill the general education requirements. That way, when you are working on completing the classes required for your major, you will already have some out of the way. The best part about your general education is you have a lot of options and you can take classes that sound interesting, or related to your major. Do not ever sign up for a class because of its convenience because it will not help your major and you will not be engrossed. By the end of completing your general education you should know your major and have enjoyed most of the classes you took.

After you choose your major, you need to remember one very important thing. Your major is *your* major. This means you will deal with people who will tell you what they think you should study, or what they want you to study. You might deal with people who say you look like you would be a good teacher and tell you to change your major. Do not be easily influenced by these people. Kathy once told me she wanted me to study business so I could make a bunch of money and buy her a house. That suggestion was not about me and if you feel the major someone wants you to study is for their benefit, then you should not do it. However, you should listen to the Als and Lauras of the world because they will give you good advice about your major and it will be beneficial for you and not them. These people are the ones I mentioned earlier in Chapter 1 and I highly recommend discussing your major and your plans after college with them frequently.

In sum, you should study something you like, or make it to where you can still be involved in what you like after you finish college. Remember you do not have to become a philosopher just because you majored in philosophy. That is ok. It is your degree that is important on your resume and an advertising agency cares more about you finishing college than knowing you can tell them the difference between egoism and utilitarianism. Pay attention to what you take for your general education classes and try to make them applicable to the requirements for your major. Moreover, seek guidance from your support system about your major and advising from a college counselor also.

CHAPTER 9

PREPARING FOR GRADUATION

I remember visiting Diana's family on the holidays and telling the same story about how college was going to the ten people who asked me at the family gatherings. At first, you tell them things like how you just chose your major, or took your writing test. Then as the four years of college continue, you find you are almost done and finally say to someone, "Oh, this is my last year." I cannot even begin to describe how saying that feels, so I am just going to let you experience it yourself.

Getting to that day takes a lot of work, and another one of those checklists I talked about in the Chapter 3. The first step you need to take is figuring out everything you need to do to graduate. For me, I had to complete 120 units, 45 of the units needed to be from my major, I needed to complete three courses that were in the same subject cluster, complete a writing exam, complete this weird research course sponsored by the library, meet with an advisor to make sure I did everything, file for graduation and pay a fee. All this work takes a while, so you need to keep track of where you are in the process.

As I mentioned in Chapter 8, try and take general education classes in your major that way you can use them later to meet your graduation requirements. You will have to take classes from diverse sections like math, English, cultural studies and others. Keep your list that has the number of classes you must take from the sections handy. It will feel great to cross more courses off this list at the end of each semester/quarter. After you finish your general education, you can focus on the requirements for your major, which includes another checklist. You will get to experience the positive, abundant feelings of crossing courses off that list too. You may have to take three classes that are within a cluster. This means you must choose a subject cluster that you like, hopefully works well with your major and take three courses in it to fulfill another requirement. I ended up taking this obscure Asian Studies cluster, which was efficient since once of the courses was an anthropology one I could use to help complete my major classes checklist. These checklists will help you make sure you are on track to graduate on time and you have done everything you need to do, so do not lose them.

If you go to a California State University, you will have to fulfill a writing requirement. You can do this by passing a writing exam, or by taking a class that meets the requirement. I suggest you take this test, or class as soon as you can. The main reason is that if you fail the test, you have time to complete the requirement in another way. It is also good to do this so that you are not scrambling during your senior year to finish everything.

Once you complete all your graduation requirements, or will be finishing them that semester/quarter, meet with the appropriate person who has to sign off on you graduating. For me, I had to have the dean of the anthropology department sign my form for graduation. This person will confirm you have fulfilled all the requirements, or will complete them that final semester/quarter and then sign a form for you. It sounds like a very simple and quick task, but as with the others, do not wait until the day it is due to finish it.

Getting to your last semester/quarter of college and graduating takes time, so make sure you give yourself enough of it. Keep checklists of the tasks you need to complete and the courses you need to take. Graduating is a huge achievement you will celebrate, but be sure to also celebrate the small achievements that lead up to your graduation. A celebration outing for ice cream when you finish a semester/quarter, or that writing exam will give you a boost you need to continue and get you excited for the next task on your list. Always celebrate the small moments and always know where you are in your journey to finishing your degree.

PART 3

POST-COLLEGE YEARS

CHAPTER 10

GRADUATE SCHOOL

I decided to go to graduate school when I was about 13 years old when I found out the type of archaeologist I once wanted to be needed a PhD. I am now happy to say I finished graduate school in 2014. Not everyone needs to go to graduate school though and certainly not everyone knows they want to go when they are 13.

The counselor who wrote the financial aid letter I mentioned earlier told me to start thinking of graduate school right before junior year started and she was correct. Junior year of college is the perfect time. When you are a junior, you will know yourself well and, most of all, know if you want and can go to school for an additional two or more years. A lot of people do not want to extend their college career, and that is totally fine if you fall into that category. You need to know your major when you are a junior also, and this is when you can investigate if the only jobs in your field require a graduate degree as I have previously mentioned. If you know you need to go to graduate school, or want to go, then you will need to go through another and much more difficult application process.

Graduate school applications are much more serious than the ones you completed for your undergraduate degree. The usual requirements are the general information application, a statement of purpose, a personal statement, three letters of recommendation, an exam and your transcripts. As with your previous applications, know who you are as an applicant and apply to schools you qualify for. The minimum GPA for a graduate school is usually a 3.0, so during your junior year, make sure you keep your GPA high, or do what you can to raise it. Be sure to also follow the same techniques of giving yourself enough time and writing your statements honestly.

The biggest change you will find when applying to graduate school, or at least thinking about it, is you need to know exactly what you want to do. You will need to know the area in your field you want to write a thesis about. Figuring this out may be easy, but it will take you a lot of time to find the university that is right for you. You will need to find a university that has someone on the faculty in your area. For example, I did not apply to San Francisco State University because I wanted to write about the Philistines from the Bronze Age and there are no professors there who could have helped me do it. Spend some time looking at different universities and figuring out where you would like to go. You may be able to slightly switch what you want to study in graduate school. For me, I started graduate school as an archaeologist and changed to applied anthropology, but not every university will let you do this. Remember how I told you only being accepted by this school was good? It was good because I could change my subfield, but the other schools may not have let me do it.

The greatest piece of advice about graduate school Al and Laura gave me was to take more than one year off before going. Unfortunately, I did not take their advice and had to work a lot more than anyone should while they are pursuing their master's degree. I highly recommend taking at least two years off before you go to graduate school so that you can save money. Taking time off can give you more time to create a better application, find the right schools and decide what you want to study. Taking time off can also help you decide which type of graduate program to enter. You have the option of going straight into a PhD program where you get a master's degree along the way, or apply to a master's degree program. Some people choose a master's program and then take more time off before getting a PhD, or stop at the master's. It is up to you on what you choose, but do as much research as you can to understand what you want to commit to and what you would like to do since the number of years is different for PhD and a master's degree.

These factors relating to your major and what you want should be considered before you make the choice to go to graduate school. Begin to think about these during your junior year and as the time passes, you can reflect on them more and make a better decision about if your future includes graduate school.

CHAPTER 11

YOUR CAREER

Three months after I finished graduate school, I received two offer letters, but it took immense time and effort. I spent many days on job boards and applied to jobs I liked and felt qualified for. As you begin your post-graduation job search, I highly recommend the websites listed in Appendix 6. I found my current job using Indeed.com, but there are some things which happened since taking the job I feel necessary to write about.

Remember how I wrote previously you warrant love from your support system, or the new life you received when you moved away? Another thing you deserve is the job you worked hard for during college. Those two offer letters I just told you about had radically different salaries. One I felt I earned and the other I did not. Al and Laura knew this and told me. I will always appreciate their straightforwardness even though it can sometimes be uncomfortable. The most shocking thing for me was that what was offered to me was greater than anything I ever expected, or felt I had earned. To be completely honest, I signed that offer letter with the idea I was not fit for it, and only signed it because there was no way I could live off the salary of the other. If this situation happens to you, sign the one you feel like you did not earn because you probably did earn it. In talking to many first-generation students, it is likely the job, or life we have post-graduation astounds us. It is bigger than we ever could have dreamed of when living in our small apartments with our shared bedrooms. After all, it is hard to dream about something you never believed you could have, or even knew existed. I recall thinking to myself when I was young about what it would mean to have "made it." Growing up the way I did made me come to believe that being able to afford Jif peanut butter instead of a generic brand and Pilot G2 pens instead of cheap ones would establish I was successful. I was close-minded, in a sense, to the possibilities of what is out there, and thought Jif and Pilot G2 pens were as big as prosperity could be. If you feel this way, you can work through it as I did. Sign the offer letter you feel is too big because your future is brighter than you imagined.

Something that often happens to first-generation students, including myself, when they are in college is this feeling of not belonging. They are surrounded by people bragging about where their parents went to school and we are standing there wondering if we have a place among them. We do belong there and it is amazing many of us even made it to college given our past circumstances. Beyond the offer letter issue existed the continued belief of not belonging. I would sometimes sit in meetings and feel like my current company could have someone who went to a more prestigious school, or had better transcripts, or a better thesis. The list goes on and on. I have sat in conference rooms across from people wearing Stanford sweatshirts and asked myself why I was sitting there too. Why did they hire *me*? The fact is, going to college and being the first one to do it is the greatest achievement I have. The single greatest thing I have done. I belong in every single meeting that comes across my calendar and you will too. You will probably sit across from people wearing Ivy League shirts, hats and sweatshirts. This does not make you reprehensible, nor does it define you. The college you attend is not the greatest thing about you. Your entire career is ahead of you and is what to look forward to.

As first-generation students, as with everyone, we are not where we came from. We are who we have become and who we will one day grow into. We are the people who deserve jobs and lives we never knew were possible. The people who sit in quarterly meetings wearing San Francisco State University shirts with no shame because going to college was a great feat.

CONCLUSION

I want to end this book by telling you a few things I learned a lot later in my life than I wish I would have. A couple of them are pieces of advice I have been given, but most of them are regrets relating to the way I wish I would have handled my journey to and through my four years of college. The first thing is that your life is not entirely made up of who you were and where you come from. You are not your parents and you do not have to become your parents. You will add and better your life once you begin college and if you work hard enough, you will probably not always be as poor as you were. I once read an article about a first-generation student who said he spends more time at conferences talking to the waiters than the other conference attendees. This is because he had to wait tables to pay for college and does not feel like he is one of his peers working on a degree. There is nothing wrong with talking to the waiters, but this student never felt like he could talk to his academic peers. He was holding himself back. The article upset me because this person never believed who he now is in the present is not the same poor person he was when he started school. You are not your past and you do not have to be ashamed of growing up the way you did and working hard to get where you are if that is you. I was once living in a household where the word broke was used frequently, and the only time I have had to use that word since going to college was when I was laid off. I cannot remind you enough to understand who you are right now and to know you do belong.

Second, you are worth it and you probably deserve it. When I was transferring from Las Positas College, I did not apply to University of California, Berkeley because I did not think I deserved it. This was related to me believing I was the family I came from and not my own individual person. I thought the people who should be at Berkeley are the ones who had parents attend that school, or had GPAs better than mine. I thought they were worth it more than me. The truth is, every single human being has worth no matter who they are. You are worth going to Stanford just as much as the fifth-generation Stanford student. Do not ever tell yourself the seat at Yale is saved for someone who comes from a nicer home because you can fill that seat just as well as him or her and be just as good a student if you try. Not believing I had earned it also made it difficult for me to ask for letters of recommendation for graduate school. If you are planning on going to college, then you have earned the help you need, so do not be afraid to ask for it. When you are in college, go to professors' office hours and ask for help also. I will say it again, it is their job to help you and you do not have to earn it.

Lastly, you are not your GPA, you are a human being. It was very easy for me to get caught up in only having a 3.3 when I finished my education at San Francisco State University. I was so engulfed in disappointment, I forgot about my other achievements that spoke louder than my GPA. I disregarded the 30 or more hours a week I had to work, all the "A's" I received on research papers and volunteer work I did. Your value is not in all the grades, it is in you as a person and as soon as you realize people like you because of your humor, or kindness, or whoever it is you are, you will understand and embrace that your value is not in your GPA. Want to know the number of job interviews where my GPA came up? Zero. Being more excited about those small achievements I told you about earlier is much better and enjoyable than being excited about your GPA.

The greatest things you can do during college are know you are more than a first-generation student, be the best student that you can, reward yourself, ask for help and treat yourself well. I guarantee they will make the long, tough, rewarding, intimidating, exciting and joyous college experience more than just four years or more you need to get over with. Your time in college is more than a piece of paper you get to hang on your wall, so do not treat it that way. Give yourself what you need and do whatever it takes to get what you need especially when you do not think you deserve it. You are worth it, so go get it.

APPENDICES

APPENDIX 1
COLLEGE APPLICATION WEBSITES
BY STATE AND DISTRICT

- **Alabama**
  - ☐ Auburn University: auburn.edu/admissions
  - ☐ University of Alabama: gobama.ua.edu/apply
- **Alaska**
  - ☐ University of Alaska Anchorage:
    uaa.alaska.edu/admissions
  - ☐ University of Alaska Fairbanks:
    uaf.edu/admissions
  - ☐ University of Alaska Southeast:
    uas.alaska.edu/admissions
- **Arizona**
  - ☐ Arizona State University: students.asu.edu/apply
  - ☐ University of Arizona: arizona.edu/how-to-apply
- **Arkansas**
  - ☐ University of Arkansas: uark.edu/admissions
- **California**
  - ☐ California State University Campuses:
    csumentor.edu/AdmissionApp
  - ☐ Stanford University: stanford.edu/admission/
  - ☐ University of California Campuses:
    admissions.universityofcalifornia.edu
  - ☐ University of Southern California: admit.usc.edu
- **Colorado**
  - ☐ Colorado State University:
    admissions.colostate.edu
  - ☐ University of Colorado: colorado.edu/admissions
  - ☐ University of Denver: du.edu/apply/admission/

- **Connecticut**
  - ☐ University of Connecticut: uconn.edu/admissions
  - ☐ Yale University: yale.edu/admissions
- **Delaware**
  - ☐ University of Delaware: udel.edu/apply/undergraduate-admissions
- **Florida**
  - ☐ Florida State University: admissions.fsu.edu
  - ☐ University of Florida: admissions.ufl.edu
  - ☐ University of Miami: welcome.miami.edu/admissions
  - ☐ University of South Florida: usf.edu/admissions
- **Georgia**
  - ☐ Emory University: apply.emory.edu
  - ☐ Georgia Institute of Technology: admission.gatech.edu
  - ☐ Georgia State University: admissions.gsu.edu
  - ☐ University of Georgia: admissions.uga.edu
- **Hawaii**
  - ☐ University of Hawaii: manoa.hawaii.edu/admissions
- **Idaho**
  - ☐ Idaho State University: isu.edu/apply
  - ☐ University of Idaho: uidaho.edu/admissions
- **Illinois**
  - ☐ Illinois Institute of Technology: admissions.iit.edu
  - ☐ Loyola University Chicago: luc.edu/admission.shtml
  - ☐ Northwestern University: northwestern.edu/admissions
  - ☐ University of Chicago: collegeadmissions.uchicago.edu
  - ☐ University of Illinois, Chicago: admissions.uic.edu

- University of Illinois, Urbana-Champaign: admissions.illinois.edu
- **Indiana**
  - Indiana State University: indstate.edu/admissions
  - Purdue University: purdue.edu/purdue/admissions
  - University of Indiana: admissions.indiana.edu
  - University of Notre Dame: admissions.nd.edu
- **Iowa**
  - Iowa State University: admissions.iastate.edu
  - University of Iowa: admissions.uiowa.edu
- **Kansas**
  - Kansas State University: k-state.edu/admissions
  - University of Kansas: admissions.ku.edu
- **Kentucky**
  - University of Kentucky: uky.edu/Admission
- **Louisiana**
  - Louisiana State University: lsu.edu/admission
  - Tulane University: admission.tulane.edu
- **Maine**
  - University of Maine System: maine.edu/admissions-aid
- **Maryland**
  - Johns Hopkins University: apply.jhu.edu
  - University of Maryland: admissions.umd.edu
- **Massachusetts**
  - Boston College: bc.edu/admission
  - Boston University: bu.edu/admissions
  - Harvard University: college.harvard.edu/admissions
  - Massachusetts Institute of Technology: mitadmissions.org
  - Northeastern University: northeastern.edu/admissions

- ☐ Tufts University: admissions.tufts.edu/
- ■ **Michigan**
  - ☐ Michigan State University: admissions.msu.edu
  - ☐ Michigan Technological University: mtu.edu/admissions
  - ☐ University of Michigan: admissions.umich.edu
- ■ **Minnesota**
  - ☐ University of Minnesota: admissions.tc.umn.edu
- ■ **Mississippi**
  - ☐ Mississippi State University: admissions.msstate.edu
  - ☐ University of Mississippi: admissions.olemiss.edu
- ■ **Missouri**
  - ☐ Missouri University of Science and Technology: futurestudents.mst.edu
  - ☐ University of Missouri: admissions.missouri.edu
  - ☐ Washington University in St. Louis: admissions.wustl.edu
- ■ **Montana**
  - ☐ Montana State University: montana.edu/admissions
  - ☐ University of Montana: admissions.umt.edu
- ■ **Nebraska**
  - ☐ University of Nebraska: admissions.unl.edu
- ■ **Nevada**
  - ☐ University of Nevada: unr.edu/admissions
- ■ **New Hampshire**
  - ☐ Dartmouth College: admissions.dartmouth.edu
  - ☐ University of New Hampshire: admissions.unh.edu
- ■ **New Jersey**
  - ☐ New Jersey Institute of Technology: njit.edu/admissions
  - ☐ Princeton University: admission.princeton.edu

- Rutgers University: admissions.rutgers.edu
- **New Mexico**
  - University of New Mexico: admissions.unm.edu
- **New York**
  - Binghamton University: binghamton.edu/admissions
  - City University of New York: cuny.edu/admissions
  - Clarkson University: clarkson.edu/admissions
  - Columbia University: undergrad.admissions.columbia.edu
  - Cornell University: admissions.cornell.edu
  - Fordham University: fordham.edu/info/20063/undergraduate_admission
  - New School University: newschool.edu/admission
  - New York University: nyu.edu/admissions.html
  - Rensselaer Polytechnic Institute: admissions.rpi.edu
  - Stony Brook University: stonybrook.edu/admissions
  - Syracuse University: syr.edu/admissions
  - University of Albany-SUNY: albany.edu/admissions.php
  - University of Buffalo SUNY: admissions.buffalo.edu/apply
  - University of Rochester: enrollment.rochester.edu
  - Yeshiva University: yu.edu/admissions
- **North Carolina**
  - Duke University: admissions.duke.edu
  - North Carolina State University: admissions.ncsu.edu
  - University of North Carolina: admissions.unc.edu
  - Wake Forest University: admissions.wfu.edu/

- **North Dakota**
  - ☐ North Dakota State University: ndsu.edu/admission
  - ☐ University of North Dakota: und.edu/admissions
- **Ohio**
  - ☐ Case Western Reserve University: admission.case.edu
  - ☐ Miami University: miamioh.edu/admission
  - ☐ Ohio State University: osu.edu/futurestudents
  - ☐ Ohio University: ohio.edu/admissions
  - ☐ University of Cincinnati: uc.edu/admit
- **Oklahoma**
  - ☐ Oklahoma State University: admissions.okstate.edu
  - ☐ University of Oklahoma: ou.edu/admissions.html
  - ☐ University of Tulsa: admission.utulsa.edu
- **Oregon**
  - ☐ Oregon State University: admissions.oregonstate.edu
  - ☐ University of Oregon: admissions.uoregon.edu
- **Pennsylvania**
  - ☐ Carnegie Mellon University: admission.enrollment.cmu.edu
  - ☐ Drexel University: drexel.edu/admissions/overview
  - ☐ Lehigh University: lehigh.edu/admissions
  - ☐ Pennsylvania State University: admissions.psu.edu/
  - ☐ Temple University: admissions.temple.edu
  - ☐ University of Pennsylvania: admissions.upenn.edu
  - ☐ University of Pittsburgh: pitt.edu/admissions
- **Rhode Island**
  - ☐ Brown University: brown.edu/admission
  - ☐ University of Rhode Island: web.uri.edu/admission/

- **South Carolina**
  - ☐ Clemson University: clemson.edu/admissions
  - ☐ University of South Carolina: sc.edu/admissions
- **South Dakota**
  - ☐ South Dakota State University: sdstate.edu/office-admissions
  - ☐ University of South Dakota: usd.edu/admissions
- **Tennessee**
  - ☐ University of Tennessee: admissions.utk.edu/
  - ☐ Vanderbilt University: admissions.vanderbilt.edu/
- **Texas**
  - ☐ Baylor University: baylor.edu/admissions
  - ☐ Rice University: rice.edu/admission-aid.shtml
  - ☐ Southern Methodist University: smu.edu/admission
  - ☐ Texas A&M University: admissions.tamu.edu
  - ☐ University of Houston: uh.edu/admissions
  - ☐ University of Texas at Austin: admissions.utexas.edu
  - ☐ University of Texas at Dallas: utdallas.edu/admissions
- **Utah**
  - ☐ Brigham Young University: admissions.byu.edu
  - ☐ University of Utah: admissions.utah.edu/apply
- **Vermont**
  - ☐ University of Vermont: uvm.edu/admissions
- **Virginia**
  - ☐ College of William & Mary: wm.edu/admission
  - ☐ George Mason University: gmu.edu/admissions-aid
  - ☐ University of Virginia: admission.virginia.edu/
  - ☐ Virginia Commonwealth University: ugrad.vcu.edu
  - ☐ Virginia Polytechnic University: admissions.vt.edu

- **Washington**
  - ☐ University of Washington: admit.washington.edu/apply
  - ☐ Washington State University: admission.wsu.edu
- **Washington D.C.**
  - ☐ American University: american.edu/admissions
  - ☐ Georgetown University: uadmissions.georgetown.edu
  - ☐ George Washington University: undergraduate.admissions.gwu.edu
  - ☐ Howard University: howard.edu/admission
- **West Virginia**
  - ☐ West Virginia University: admissions.wvu.edu
- **Wisconsin**
  - ☐ Marquette University: marquette.edu/admissions
  - ☐ University of Wisconsin-Madison: wisc.edu/admissions
- **Wyoming**
  - ☐ University of Wyoming: uwyo.edu/admissions
- **Multiple Universities with One Application**
  - ☐ coalitionforcollegeaccess.org
  - ☐ commonapp.org

APPENDIX 2
FINANCIAL AID

- **Government Financial Aid**
  - ☐ fafsa.ed.gov
- **Scholarships**
  - ☐ fastweb.com
  - ☐ zinch.com
  - ☐ cappex.com
  - ☐ scholarships.com
  - ☐ nextstudent.com
  - ☐ scholarshipexperts.com
  - ☐ Consider scholarships offered by the school you choose to attend
  - ☐ Consider scholarships for your race, religion and the like

APPENDIX 3
STANDARDIZED TEST PREPARATION

- Xiggi Method: blog.prepscholar.com/the-definitive-guide-to-the-xiggi-method-for-sat-prep
- Kaplan SAT Course: kaptest.com/sat
- Kaplan ACT Course: kaptest.com/act
- SAT Books:
- *The Official SAT Study Guide* by College Board
    - ☐ *SAT Premier 2017* by Kaplan
- ACT Books:
    - ☐ *The Official ACT Prep Guide* by ACT
    - ☐ *ACT 2016-2017 Strategies, Practice and Review with 6 Practice Tests: Online + Book* by Kaplan
- GRE Course: kaptest.com/gre
- GRE Books:
    - ☐ *Barron's GRE, 21ˢᵗ Edition* by Sharon Weiner Green M.A. And Ira K. Wolf Ph.D.

APPENDIX 4
APPS AND WEBSITES
FOR NOTES AND
ASSIGNMENTS

- **Evernote** has a website and apps. It is my favorite tool for note taking because my notes would sync across all my devices—iPhone, iPad and MacBook. I ended up writing some of my thesis at the beach using Evernote on my iPhone and edited it when I got home.
- **Easybib.com** is an amazing website for quickly creating bibliographies for essays. Saves a ton of time.
- **Studyblue** has a website and apps to creating digital flash cards. The flashcards can also be shared with others, so you can collaborate with people in your study groups to create cards for different sections of a class. The mobile apps are great for studying while commuting.
- **Dropbox** has websites and apps and is a great place to store all your files in case your computer ever breaks down. Your files can also sync across all your devices.
- **Apps by Readdle**
  - ☐ **Calendars** is an app that I've found to have a cleaner design than the calendar apps that come pre-installed on phones. This app can connect with Google Calendar and iCal.
  - ☐ **Documents** is an app that is perfect for saving articles and other files that are required reading for classes instead of printing hundreds of pages a semester/quarter.
  - ☐ **PDF Expert** is an app that allows for annotating and highlighting PDF files. Again, like Documents, this app allows for not printing PDF files that are required reading for classes.

APPENDIX 5
JOB SEARCH WEBSITES

- indeed.com
- angel.co (for startup jobs)
- linkedin.com
    - ☐ You should be sure to create a LinkedIn account sooner than later since this is how you will connect with those you work with or meet at networking events.
- craigslist.org
- monster.com
- simplyhired.com
- Handshake app
    - ☐ This app connects college graduates with employers in a seamless way. Their work is dedicated to matching students and graduates with employers using data no matter what the student studied and where they are located. you work with or meet at networking events.

RESOURCES

"2016 Facts About the CSU." 2016 Facts About the CSU. California State University, 14 Apr. 2016. Web. 13 Feb. 2017.

Buyagawan, Nicole. "Facing the Gap: The Struggles of First Generation College Students." Mar. 2013

Cantarella, Marcia Y. "Being Black and Fitting in at College." *The Huffington Post.* http://www.huffingtonpost.com/marcia-y-cantarella-phd/being-black-and-fitting-i_b_8631182.html, 18 May 2016.

Damouras, Jennifer. "My Challenges as a First-Generation College Student." http://www.huffingtonpost.com/jennifer-damouras/my-challenges-as-a-firstg_b_7097782.html 2015.

Ueland, Brenda. *If You Want to Write.* Saint Paul: Graywolf, 1987.

Zhang, Fred. "What Is a Good ACT Score? A Bad ACT Score? An Excellent ACT Score?" *PrepScholar,* http://blog.prepscholar.com/what-is-a-good-sat-score-a-bad-sat-score-an-excellent-sat-score 14 Nov. 2014.

Zhang, Fred. "What Is a Good SAT Score? A Bad SAT Score? An Excellent SAT Score?" *PrepScholar,* http://blog.prepscholar.com/what-is-a-good-act-score-a-bad-act-score-an-excellent-act-score 2016.

ACKNOWLEDGEMENTS

There are many people I would like to thank since they made this book possible. Before I mention those who directly helped me during my time of writing and editing, I want to tell you about some of the people who have made an impact on my education and employment because I would not be who I am today without them. I have been lucky enough to have amazing teachers and professors throughout my life. My sixth-grade language arts and history teacher was more invested in my education than anyone I had encountered before. It was in her class where I fell in love with anthropology and do not feel I would be in the career I am had she not made the subjects she taught as interesting as she did. During my undergraduate education, I was taught well by my professors for anthropology theory, ancient archaeology, Greek culture and Far East archaeology. During graduate school, my thesis advisor was a rock for me and I have no idea how he could manage all the theses he read. Without any of these educators, my times of studying, writing papers and discovering more about myself through lectures and readings would have lacked something I needed to continue pursuing my education on the days life felt unmanageable.

I have been blessed with amazing employers as well as teachers. While in college, I had an amazing boss—Jayme at Raley's. I am grateful to her for working around my school schedule and being good with my education being the most important thing in my life. Jayme taught me all sorts of small things while bagging bread, and slicing cakes that seemed insignificant at the time, but have helped me in the way I relate to people in my job today and how I break down projects to make them successful. Every once in a while, I hear her in my head saying, "Katelyn, work smarter, not harder!" Regarding my work after graduate school, my bosses, Aaron and Christian, made me feel like I belonged in my job as a researcher and in the tech world, which is something I never thought I would feel due to my background. They believed in me more than I ever did and made me feel valued as I was writing this book outside of work. Aaron loves all his employees as if they are his children and I dearly miss working under him. Without them, the career section of this book would be empty. Thank you to all of you.

The most important person behind this book, besides my publisher, is Al. When I told him my idea for the book, he made me send the Prologue to him four days later (are you kidding me?!). Without his loving pressure, and rigid yet needed feedback, this book would not exist. The support from Laura, Erin, and Kevin is, of course, next on the list. I have a lot of great friends in my life, who all had positive and necessary reactions while I journeyed through writing and editing this book. Therefore, I have to thank Anamaria, Kathryn, Kara, Ricardo, Wendy, Tracy and Rachel. My brother, who has become a best friend the last two years, and his girlfriend have also been supports for me.

To my publisher and editor, Megan, there are not enough thank yous I could say to express my gratitude for all the time you put into this book. I have no idea how you did it while raising two kids, being a full-time pastor, traveling frequently and your work as a chaplain. When you sat across from me at that vegetarian restaurant and told me you would help me for free, I was astounded and I am grateful to see this book on paper between a front and back cover.

Noelle, the one who this book is dedicated to, was my best friend for five straight years before we both went our separate ways after high school. She was the first peer I discussed college with in a serious way. We spent a lot of time talking about graduate degrees and, unfortunately, she passed away before she could attain one. Her raw emotion she showed to me and everyone who has met her is something I will probably never see again in anyone. We could always pick up right where we left off even if we had not spoken for months. I miss her dearly and there is no one on earth who I feel is a better fit to have a book about education, struggle, and victory dedicated to. I love you, buddy, and thank you for everything.

11553864R10058

Made in the USA
Monee, IL
12 September 2019